I0814388

THE LITTLE BOOK OF DUMPLINGS

Bundles of Love from Around the World

Other Books by Lynda Balslev

The Little Book of Fika
The Little Book of Whiskey
The Little Book of Cheese and Charcuterie

THE LITTLE BOOK OF DUMPLINGS

Bundles of Love from Around the World

Lynda Balslev

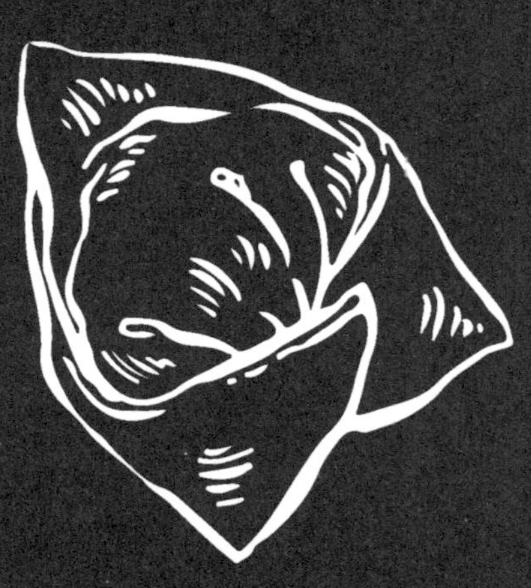

CONTENTS

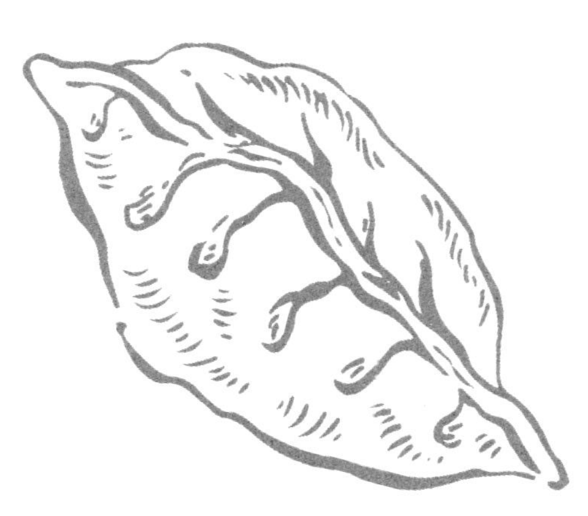

INTRODUCTION
EVERYONE LOVES A DUMPLING

This book is a tribute to the world of dumplings. From crispy Chinese wontons to spicy Indian samosas and cheesy Polish pierogi to sweet German knödel, nearly every culture has its own version of a beloved dumpling. These flavorful bundles, wrapped or rolled in dough and prepared with love, are a global culinary treasure.

What makes dumplings so universally loved is their power to bring people together. They are more than just sustenance; they are reflections of heritage and identity. Each dumpling tells a story of resourcefulness and ingenuity, of families and tradition, of holidays celebrated and recipes passed down through generations. The act of making dumplings is a ritual to be savored—a labor of love for which families and communities gather, hands busy with rolling, filling, and folding. They tell stories, cherish memories, and finish the process with a joyous meal meant to be shared together.

No matter where you are from or how you prepare them, dumplings are a unifying comfort food—a humble and delicious reminder that we're more alike than we are different. Let this book be your guide to dumplings—and their traditions—from around the globe and how to make them.

Enjoy—the world is your dumpling.

Food is everything we are. It's an extension of nationalist feeling, ethnic feeling, your personal history, your province, your region, your tribe, your grandma. It's inseparable from those from the get-go.

—ANTHONY BOURDAIN

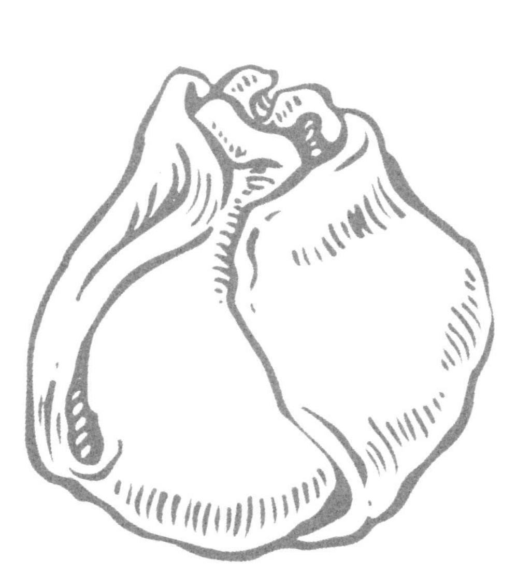

ORIGIN

Dumplings are ancient. It's believed that the earliest evidence of a wrapped dumpling traces to China during the Eastern Han Dynasty, which lasted from 25 AD to 220 AD. Legend has it that a Chinese physician created dumplings to provide sustenance to the populace during the harsh winter months.

Since then the tradition of dumplings has crossed borders and sailed across the globe, via the Silk Road into Europe and beyond to Africa and the Americas. Dumplings' tidy self-packaging enabled them to withstand long journeys, providing ideal portable sustenance for soldiers, explorers, and laborers alike. Over generations, migrating settlers introduced their dumpling traditions to their adopted new homes. With every new exposure, dumplings were absorbed into the local cuisine, embracing available and humble ingredients.

Their popularity is no surprise. Dumplings are simple comfort food. This simplicity drove their universal appeal, and over time dumplings transcended their role as mere sustenance. Families and communities of all means gathered and shared in the process of making and eating dumplings. They evolved into symbols of joy, celebration, and community and represented traditional familial bonds and cultural identity.

The word *dumpling* has uncertain origins, but the term emerged in English by the seventeenth century to describe small lumps of steamed or poached dough. One theory suggests it may have come from the Low German word *dampfn*, meaning "to steam," or from the Dutch word *damp*, which also relates to steaming.

Food is central to our sense of identity. The way any given human group eats helps it assert its diversity, hierarchy, and organization, but also, at the same time, both its oneness and the otherness of whoever eats differently. Food is also central to individual identity, in that any given human individual is constructed, biologically, psychologically, and socially by the foods he/she chooses to incorporate.

—CLAUDE FISCHLER

DUMPLING BASICS

Dumplings generally consist of a starchy dough or wrapper that encases a filling. They can be savory or sweet; are often steamed, boiled, baked, or fried; and contain an endless variety of fillings. They can be served as a starter, a snack, a main dish, or a dessert.

DOUGH

Most dumpling doughs rely on flour and water for the wrapper. Eggs and fat (butter or oil) are often added to enrich and soften the dough. Depending on the region and local ingredients, other starches, such as potato or corn, can be used as well.

TIPS

When working with the dough and wrappers, cover any unused portions with a damp towel to prevent drying out.

Don't overwork the dough. Overworking the dough can make it tough and difficult to work with.

FILLING

The heart of a dumpling is the filling. It can be savory or sweet, meaty or vegetarian. It should have a balance of flavors and texture. The seasoning can be as simple as salt and pepper or amplified with aromatics and spices.

TIPS

For medium-size dumplings, a general ratio of filling to wrappers is approximately 2 cups of filling to about 24 wrappers.

Finely chop the ingredients so they will fit compactly in the wrapper without poking through the dough. When sautéing the filling ingredients, make sure to cook off the excess liquid to prevent the dumplings becoming soggy (except in soup dumplings).

Fillings can often be prepared in advance and refrigerated until wrapping. In fact, it's often better to allow the filling to rest for at least 30 minutes to allow the flavors to develop.

Use cornstarch or flour to dust the work surface for rolling the wrappers (don't over-flour or the dough will be too dry).

Have all the ingredients ready when you are ready to assemble the dumplings.

Start with placing a little less filling in each wrapper to make your first attempts easier.

FOLDING AND SHAPING

Begin with basic folding techniques, such as half-moon shapes. The more you practice, the better you'll become at assembling dumplings.

TIPS

Use a 3½ to 4-inch cookie cutter to cut square wrappers into round shapes.

When wrapping, have a small bowl of water at the ready to dip your finger in to seal the edges of the wrapper.

Tightly seal the edges and press out any air pockets. This prevents the dumpling breaking apart while cooking. A firm seal will also prevent any leakage.

Store-bought wrappers are generally less sticky and smaller than homemade recipes specify. Note that if using store-bought wrappers, your dumpling yield will be higher.

Dumplings not only refers to starchy wraps that encase a filling but also applies to steamed or boiled morsels of dough that are often rolled into round shapes and served in sauces, soups, or compotes. In Europe, where potatoes are abundant, potato starch is often used to make round dumplings, or knödel. In African and Caribbean cuisine, cassava, plantains, or yams are used to make dumplings called fufu, and in the Americas, maize or corn is a revered starch often used for dumplings.

The common themes throughout are simplicity, stretching resources, and making use of humble available ingredients. The outcome is a cherished comfort food passed down through generations.

SHAPES

HALF-MOON/CRESCENT

This is a simple, basic shape used for Chinese jiaozi (potstickers), Japanese gyoza, Korean mandu, Nepalese momo, and Polish pierogi.

Place a spoonful of filling on a round dumpling wrapper. Fold the wrapper in half to enclose the filling. Pinch or pleat the edges to seal.

BASIC WONTON (BONNET)

Use this basic wonton shape for Chinese wontons, Siberian pelmeni, Ashkenazi kreplach, and Turkish manti.

Place a spoonful of filling on a square dumpling wrapper. Fold the wrapper in half to enclose the filling and form a rectangle, seam side up. Pinch the edges to seal. Bend the two corners of the folded edge toward each other to form a round shape.

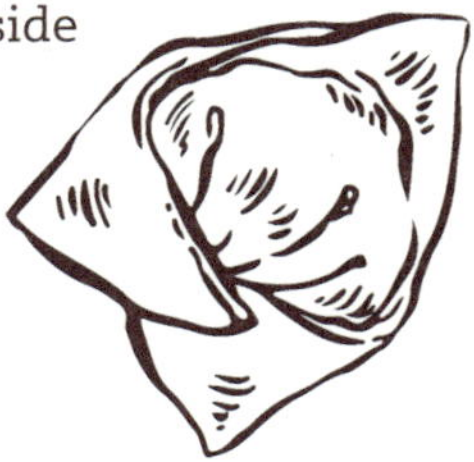

WONTON DIAMOND

This shape is best for deep-frying.

Place a spoonful of filling on a square dumpling wrapper. Fold the wrapper in half diagonally to enclose the filling and form a triangle. Bend the two opposite corners toward each other to form a round shape. Pinch the edges to seal.

SIU MAI

Use this shape as a steamed alternative to Chinese jiaozi (potstickers) or wontons or Japanese gyoza.

Use a 3½-inch round egg-enriched wonton wrapper. Cup the wrapper in your hand. Place the filling in the middle of the wrapper. Fold up the sides, pressing in and around the filling, while leaving the top open.

BAO

Use this shape for Georgian khinkali and Chinese xiao long bao, or soup dumplings. These dumplings have a cinched purselike shape with pleats encircling the filling to seal and form a stem or handle.

Place a spoonful of filling in the center of a thin round dumpling wrapper. Lift and pleat the edges around the filling, pinching each pleat closed as you go. Leave a small hole at the top to allow steam to escape during cooking.

COOKING METHODS

There are several ways to cook dumplings. Dumplings can be boiled, pan-fried, steamed, baked, deep-fried, or air-fried. Each method provides a different texture and flavor.

Note that when cooking a raw meat filling, the internal temperature of the cooked dumpling should register 165°F with a meat thermometer. When cooking a raw seafood filling, the internal temperature of the cooked dumpling should register 145°F with a meat thermometer.

BOIL

Boiled dumplings are soft and tender and have a mild flavor. They are often served in soups or with a dipping sauce.

Bring a large pot of water to a gentle boil over high heat. Lower the dumplings into the gently boiling liquid to prevent them bursting. To prevent them sticking together, do not crowd the pot. Gently boil until the dumplings float to the top, then continue to cook for 2 to 4 minutes longer, depending on the filling, stirring occasionally to prevent sticking. Remove the dumplings from the water with a spider strainer or slotted spoon.

Examples of boiled dumplings are Chinese soup dumplings and wontons, Georgian khinkali, Siberian pelmeni, Polish pierogi, Ukrainian varenyky, Ashkenazi kreplach, German knödel, Italian gnudi, Swedish kroppkakor, Turkish manti, and South African souskluitjies.

PAN-FRY

Pan-fried dumplings are first pan-fried and then finished by steaming so that they're crisp on the bottom and moist on top. Fry the dumplings in a pan lightly coated with vegetable oil over medium-high heat until golden brown on the bottom, 2 to 3 minutes. Carefully add about 1/4 cup cold water to the pan (it will spatter). Cover the pan and decrease the heat to medium. Steam the dumplings until fully cooked, 2 to 8 minutes, depending on the filling, then remove the lid and continue to cook until the water has evaporated.

Examples of pan-fried dumplings are Chinese jiaozi (potstickers), Japanese gyoza, preboiled Polish pierogi, and Ashkenazi kreplach.

STEAM

Steamed dumplings are more delicate than boiled dumplings. They have a soft and slightly chewy texture and a clean flavor. Use a bamboo steamer or lightly oil a metal steamer basket to prevent sticking or line the basket with lettuce or cabbage leaves as a buffer. Arrange the dumplings in a single layer in the basket. Steam over boiling water until the dumplings are puffed and slightly translucent and the filling is entirely cooked, 8 to 15 minutes, depending on the filling.

Examples of steamed dumplings are Chinese soup dumplings, Asian siu mai, Nepalese momo, and Siberian pelmeni.

BAKE

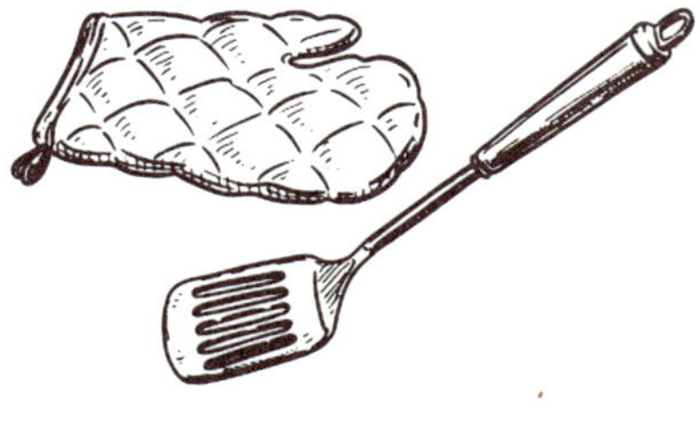

Baking is a method more frequently used for pastry-wrapped dumplings, such as samosas and empanadas, which are firm and crispy with a flaky wrapper that requires baking. Preheat your oven to 375°F (or as specified). Line a baking sheet with parchment paper. Arrange the dumplings on the baking sheet and lightly brush them with vegetable oil or an egg wash before baking, if desired. Bake until the dumplings are golden brown and the filling is entirely cooked, 20 to 25 minutes, turning once.

Examples of baked dumplings are samosas and empanadas.

DEEP-FRY

Deep-fried dumplings are crisp and crunchy. They are submerged in batches in hot (350° to 375°F) neutral oil and fried until golden brown and crisp, 2 to 5 minutes, depending on the size and filling. Use a spider strainer to remove them from the oil and place them on a plate lined with paper towels to drain the excess oil.

Examples of deep-fried dumplings are samosas, empanadas, Chinese wontons, Japanese gyoza, Korean mandu, and preboiled Polish pierogi.

AIR-FRY

Air-frying is a healthier alternative to deep-frying dumplings. Preheat your air fryer to 375°F. Lightly brush the dumplings with vegetable oil. Arrange them in the air fryer basket in a single layer without touching. Air-fry until the dumplings are fully cooked through, 8 to 12 minutes (depending on the filling), flipping once. Air-frying is also a great method to reheat or cook frozen dumplings.

Use an air fryer for fried empanadas, samosas, and Chinese wontons.

STORING AND FREEZING

Raw dumplings can be stored in the refrigerator for up to 2 days. Place them on a tray or plate without touching and cover with plastic wrap.

Cooked dumplings can be stored in the refrigerator for 2 to 3 days. Cool completely, then place in an airtight container, separated by parchment paper to prevent sticking. To reheat, steam them over boiling water for 5 to 8 minutes; pan-fry over medium heat to re-crisp and heat through, 3 to 5 minutes; air-fry at 350°F for 5 to 8 minutes; or microwave in a microwave-safe container, with a little water sprinkled over them and covered with a damp paper towel, for 1 to 2 minutes.

Dumplings freeze well. Freeze raw dumplings immediately after shaping. Place them on a flour-dusted or parchment-lined tray without touching and freeze. Once frozen, transfer the dumplings to an airtight freezer bag. Raw dumplings can be frozen for up to 3 months. Cooked dumplings can be frozen for up to 4 weeks. Reheat frozen cooked dumplings directly from the freezer.

Note that their cooking times may be slightly longer when reheating from frozen.

SPECIAL EQUIPMENT

Rolling pin

3 to 6-inch round cookie cutters

Kitchen towels

Large pot for boiling

Spider strainer or slotted spoon

Parchment paper

Bamboo steamer or metal basket steamer

Baking sheet

Skillet

Air fryer

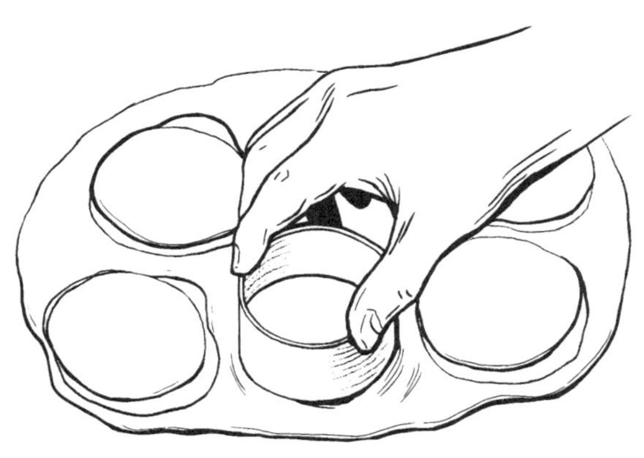

HOW TO HOST A DUMPLING PARTY

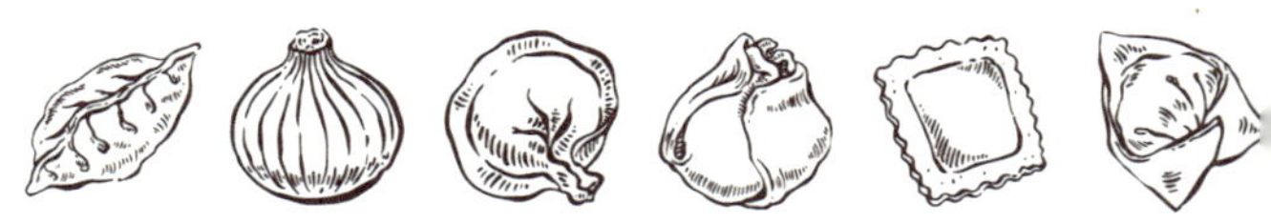

Cooking together is fun and social, with tasty benefits. Hosting a dumpling party is an interactive and festive event that allows everyone to learn and cook together and then unite around a delicious feast. Follow these tips for success!

Prepare the dough so it can rest before the party begins. Bring it to room temperature before rolling.

Prepare the fillings in advance as well. Aim for three different fillings: one meat, one shellfish, and one vegetable, such as mushroom.

Set up separate stations for each wrapping step to smooth the process: one each for rolling, stuffing, wrapping, and sealing. Have damp kitchen towels or plastic wrap ready to cover any remaining dough not being worked on.

Plan on 16 to 20 dumplings per person to allow for breakage and leftovers.

Have dipping condiments and sauces ready in advance. Make homemade sauces or purchase prepared dipping sauces, such as ponzu and sriracha, ahead of time.

Provide beverages and lay out nibbles to quell appetites. Depending on the regional inspiration of the dumplings, choose snacks that align with their regional cuisine.

Provide containers for any leftovers for guests to take home.

In many cultures, dumplings represent prosperity and good luck. Preparing dumplings is a celebration and communal activity that often brings generations together to roll and knead dough, stuff fillings, and share stories.

DOUGH RECIPES

BASIC ASIAN DUMPLING DOUGH

MAKES ABOUT 1 POUND DOUGH
(YIELDS ABOUT 24 WRAPPERS)

This basic, versatile dough is often cut into round shapes and used for dumplings that are steamed, pan-fried, or deep-fried. It can be made in a food processor or by hand. Use this recipe for wrapping Chinese jiaozi (potstickers), Japanese gyoza, Korean mandu, and Nepalese momo.

2 cups unbleached all-purpose flour

¾ cup water, very warm (130°F)

If using a food processor, place the flour in the bowl of a food processor. With the machine running, add the water in a steady stream through the feed tube until a rough dough forms. Turn off the machine and check the dough; it should hold its shape when pinched. Pulse two or three times, until the dough comes together. Do not overprocess.

CONTINUED

If making by hand, place the flour in a bowl and make a well in the center. Add the water to the well in a steady stream while stirring in the flour with a wooden spoon until the mixture is ragged.

Transfer the dough to a work surface. Knead until smooth, elastic, and slightly sticky, 2 to 3 minutes, without overworking the dough (which will make it tough). Cover the dough with plastic wrap or a damp towel and let rest at room temperature for at least 30 minutes.

When ready to shape, divide the dough into four equal pieces. Work with one piece at a time, keeping the other pieces covered with plastic wrap or a damp towel to prevent them drying out. Roll each piece into an 8-inch log. Cut slices about 1 inch thick. (Each piece should weigh about ½ ounce.)

Lightly flour a work surface, then roll each slice into a circle, 3½ to 4 inches wide and ⅛ inch thick. Use a cookie cutter to trim the edges, if desired. Gather any dough scraps together and roll into a circle. Repeat until all the scraps are used.

Use the wrappers immediately or refrigerate, stacked with a light dusting of cornstarch between each one, for up to 2 days. Or freeze with parchment paper between each wrapper for up to 1 month.

GLUTEN-FREE BASIC ASIAN DUMPLING DOUGH

MAKES ABOUT 1¼ POUNDS DOUGH
(YIELDS ABOUT 24 WRAPPERS)

This gluten-free option is an alternative to a traditional basic Asian dough. Glutinous rice flour and xanthan gum contribute to its tender texture. This dough will dry out quickly, so assemble each dumpling as soon as you roll out the dough. Keep the dough and dumplings covered with a damp towel while you assemble. Alternatively, use store-bought rice spring roll wrappers and use two wrappers per dumpling to prevent tearing.

1½ cups gluten-free flour blend

¾ cup glutinous rice flour

1½ teaspoons xanthan gum

1 cup water, at room temperature

1 teaspoon vegetable oil

Combine the flours and xanthan gum in a bowl. Add the water and oil and mix until the dough comes together. Knead the dough until smooth and elastic, 2 to 3 minutes.

Divide the dough into four equal pieces. Work with one piece at a time, keeping the other pieces covered with plastic wrap or a damp towel to prevent them drying out. Roll each piece into an 8-inch log. Cut slices about 1 inch thick. (Each slice should weigh a little more than ½ ounce.)

Lightly flour a work surface, then roll each slice into a circle, 3½ to 4 inches wide and ⅛ inch thick. Use a cookie cutter to trim the edges, if desired. Gather any dough scraps together and roll into a circle. Repeat until all the scraps are used.

WONTON EGG WRAPPER DOUGH

MAKES ABOUT 1 POUND DOUGH
(YIELDS ABOUT 24 WRAPPERS)

Wonton wrappers are enriched with egg and thinner than a basic flour wrapper. They are often square in shape and are used for dumplings that are boiled in soup or fried. Use this recipe for wrapping wontons, siu mai, kreplach, and manti.

2 cups unbleached all-purpose flour

¾ teaspoon kosher salt

1 large egg

⅓ cup water, plus more as needed

If using a food processor, place the flour and salt in the bowl of the food processor and pulse once or twice. Whisk together the egg and water in a small bowl. With the machine running, add the egg mixture through the feed tube in a steady stream and process until the mixture comes together in a sticky ball. Transfer the dough to a work surface. Knead until slightly firm, smooth, and elastic, about 2 minutes.

If making by hand, place the flour and salt in a bowl and make a well in the center. Lightly whisk together the egg and water in a small bowl. Add the egg mixture to the well in a steady stream while stirring in the flour with a wooden spoon until the mixture is ragged. Transfer the dough to a work surface. Knead until slightly firm, smooth, and elastic, about 2 minutes.

Cover the dough with plastic wrap or a damp towel and let rest at room temperature for at least 30 minutes.

Divide the dough in half. Work with one half at a time, keeping the other half covered to prevent it drying out. Lightly dust a work surface with flour or cornstarch. Roll the dough out as thin as possible, about 1/16 inch thick. Cut into 3 to 4-inch squares or use a cookie cutter to make 3 to 4-inch circles.

CONTINUED

Gather any dough scraps together and reroll into a circle. Repeat until all the scraps are used.

Use the wrappers immediately or refrigerate, stacked with cornstarch between the layers, for up to 2 days. Or freeze with parchment paper between each wrapper for up to 1 month.

BASIC EUROPEAN DUMPLING DOUGH

MAKES ABOUT 1 POUND DOUGH
(YIELDS 24 TO 30 WRAPPERS)

This soft dough includes fat, which yields a soft and sturdy wrapper for meatier dumplings. Use this dough for wrapping Georgian khinkali, Siberian pelmeni, Polish pierogi, and Ukrainian varenyky.

2 cups unbleached all-purpose flour

¾ teaspoon kosher salt

1 large egg

½ cup water, lukewarm (100°F)

1 tablespoon vegetable oil or melted butter

Whisk together the flour and salt in a large bowl. Make a well in the center and add the egg. Stir lightly with a fork while gradually adding the water and oil and continue stirring until a rough dough comes together.

CONTINUED

Lightly flour a work surface, then transfer the dough and knead until smooth and elastic, 8 to 10 minutes. If the dough is too sticky, add a little more flour. Cover the dough with plastic wrap or a damp towel and let rest at room temperature for at least 30 minutes.

When ready to shape, divide the dough into two or three equal pieces. Work with one piece at a time, keeping the other pieces covered to prevent them drying out. Lightly flour a work surface, then roll out the dough to desired thickness. Cut into desired shapes. Gather any dough scraps together and reroll into a circle. Repeat until all the scraps are used.

SOUR CREAM DUMPLING DOUGH

MAKES ABOUT 1 POUND DOUGH
(YIELDS 24 TO 30 WRAPPERS)

Sour cream adds extra richness to a basic dough. It's a popular option for pierogi wrappers. Use this dough for wrapping pierogi and for pelmeni, khinkali, and varenyky.

2 cups unbleached all-purpose flour

¾ teaspoon kosher salt

1 large egg

¼ cup sour cream

¼ cup water, lukewarm (100°F)

1 tablespoon melted butter

Whisk together the flour and salt in a bowl. Make a well in the center and add the egg and sour cream. Stir lightly with a fork while gradually adding the water and butter and continue stirring until a rough dough comes together.

CONTINUED

Lightly flour a work surface, then transfer the dough and knead until smooth and elastic, about 8 minutes. If the dough is too sticky, add a little more flour. Cover the dough with plastic wrap or a damp towel and let rest at room temperature for at least 30 minutes.

When ready to shape, divide the dough into two or three equal pieces. Work with one piece at a time, keeping the other pieces covered to prevent them drying out. Lightly flour a work surface, then roll out the dough to desired thickness. Cut into desired shapes. Gather any dough scraps together and reroll into a circle. Repeat until all the scraps are used.

DUMPLING RECIPES

ASIA

Food is maybe the only universal thing that really has the power to bring everyone together. No matter what culture, everywhere around the world, people get together to eat.

—GUY FIERI

CHINESE MUSHROOM & CABBAGE JIAOZI

MAKES ABOUT 24

Jiaozi are half-moon/crescent-shaped dumplings originally referred to as "tender ears" because they were used to treat frostbitten ears during harsh winters. They became a symbol of healing and comfort. Jiaozi can be steamed, boiled, or pan-fried. They earned the name "potstickers" because they often stick to the wok when frying.

FILLING

1 tablespoon vegetable oil

10 ounces fresh shiitake mushrooms, stems trimmed, finely chopped

1 medium carrot, grated

1½ cups shredded green cabbage

4 scallions, white and green parts separated, chopped

2 garlic cloves, minced

CONTINUED

1 tablespoon peeled, finely grated fresh ginger

¼ cup chopped cilantro leaves and tender stems

2 tablespoons soy sauce

1 teaspoon toasted sesame oil

¼ teaspoon white pepper

WRAPPERS

Basic Asian Dumpling Dough (page 21) or 24 (3½ to 4-inch) round prepared wrappers

EXTRAS

1 tablespoon vegetable or sesame oil, for pan-frying

Asian Dumpling Dipping Sauce (page 41), for serving

To make the filling, heat the oil in a skillet over medium heat. Add the mushrooms and sauté until they release their juices, about 2 minutes. Stir in the carrot, cabbage, white scallions, garlic, and ginger and sauté until fragrant and the cabbage is slightly wilted, 1 to 2 minutes. Stir in the green scallions, cilantro, soy sauce, sesame oil, and white pepper. Remove from the heat, then transfer the mixture to a bowl and let cool.

Roll out the dough as thin as possible, about ⅛ inch thick. Use a cookie cutter to cut into 3½ to 4-inch circles. Place about 1 tablespoon of the filling in the center of a wrapper and fold into a half-moon. Pinch or pleat the edges to seal. Line a tray with parchment paper or dust with flour. Set the dumpling on the tray and cover with plastic wrap or a damp towel to prevent it drying out. Repeat with the remaining filling and wrappers.

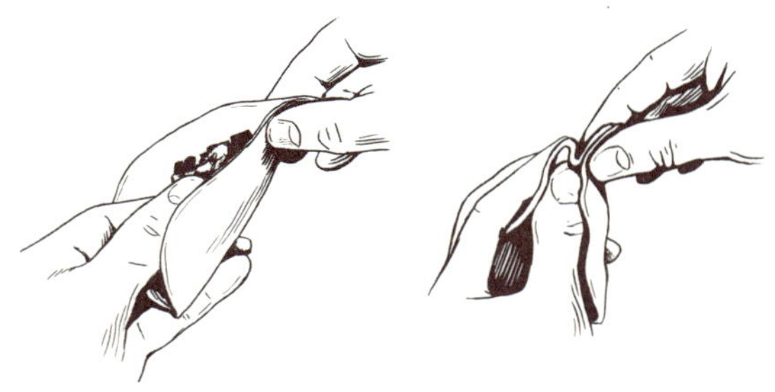

Heat the oil in a large skillet over medium-high heat. Arrange the dumplings in the pan, without overcrowding, sealed edges up. Pan-fry until golden brown on the bottom, 2 to 3 minutes. Carefully add ¼ cup water to the pan (it will spatter). Decrease the heat to medium and cover the pan. Let the dumplings steam for 2 to 3 minutes, then uncover and let any remaining water evaporate.

CONTINUED

Cooked jiaozi can be stored in the refrigerator for up to 2 days or frozen for up to 2 months. Cool completely, then place in an airtight container, separated by parchment paper to prevent sticking. Or freeze on a tray in a single layer without touching, then transfer to a freezer-safe bag or container. To reheat, steam over boiling water for 5 to 8 minutes.

Serve with Asian Dumpling Dipping Sauce.

In Chinese tradition, dumplings symbolize good luck, wealth, and prosperity. According to legend, the more dumplings you eat during Lunar New Year celebrations, the more money you will make that year.

ASIAN DUMPLING DIPPING SAUCE

MAKES ABOUT 1 CUP

½ cup soy sauce
½ cup unseasoned rice vinegar
1 large garlic clove, grated
2 teaspoons peeled, finely grated fresh ginger
1 teaspoon toasted sesame oil
½ teaspoon chili oil

Whisk together all the ingredients in a small bowl. Store at room temperature for up to 1 hour or refrigerate until use.

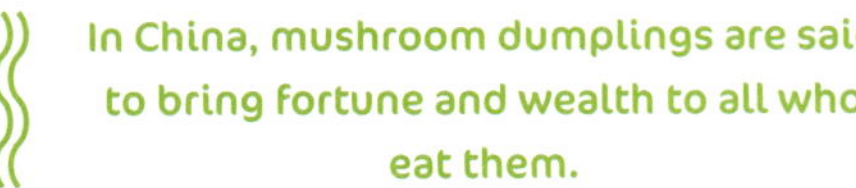

In China, mushroom dumplings are said to bring fortune and wealth to all who eat them.

SHRIMP & CHICKEN WONTONS

MAKES 24 TO 30

Wontons are traditionally made with square wrappers that are thinner than jiaozi wrappers. They are often boiled, deep-fried, or served in a soup.

FILLING

4 dried shiitake mushrooms

8 ounces shrimp, peeled, deveined, and finely chopped

8 ounces ground chicken

1 tablespoon peeled, finely chopped fresh ginger

6 scallions, chopped

2 tablespoons soy sauce

1 teaspoon toasted sesame oil

½ teaspoon kosher salt

½ teaspoon white pepper

WRAPPERS

Wonton Egg Wrapper Dough (page 26) or
24 to 30 (3½ to 4-inch) square prepared wrappers

EXTRAS

Asian Dumpling Dipping Sauce (page 41), for serving

To make the filling, place the mushrooms in a bowl of hot water to reconstitute until soft. Drain and squeeze out any liquid. Finely chop and place in a bowl. Add the remaining filling ingredients and stir until well combined. Cover and refrigerate for at least 30 minutes to allow the flavors to develop.

For the wrappers, roll out the dough as thin as possible, about 1/16 inch thick. Cut into 3½ to 4-inch squares. Gather the dough scraps into a ball and roll again until all the dough is used.

CONTINUED

Fill a small bowl with water for wetting the edges of the wonton wrappers with your fingers to seal. Place 1 teaspoon of the filling in the center of a wrapper. Fold diagonally, pressing down on the edges to seal the wrapper. Pinch the two far corners together toward the middle to make a tortellini shape. Line a tray with parchment paper or dust with flour. Set the dumpling on the tray and cover with plastic wrap or a damp towel to prevent it drying out. Repeat with the remaining filling and wrappers.

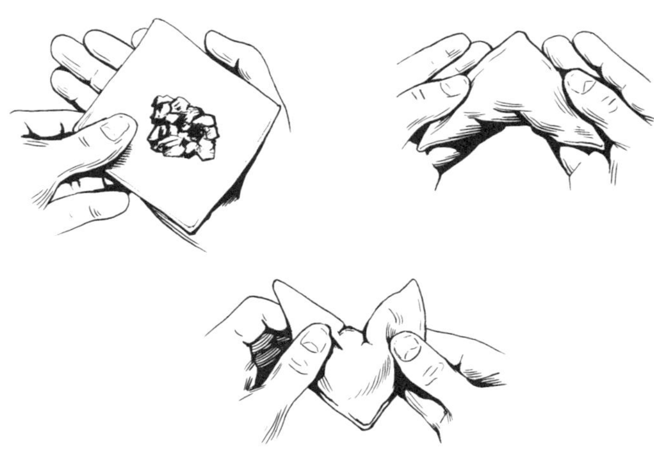

Fill a large pot with water and bring to a boil over high heat. Add the wontons and cook until they float, about 5 minutes. Carefully remove with a spider strainer and transfer to a plate.

Serve with Asian Dumpling Dipping Sauce. Alternatively, you can add them to broth for a soup.

Cooked wontons can be stored in the refrigerator for up to 2 days or frozen for up to 2 months. Cool completely, then place in an airtight container, separated by parchment paper to prevent sticking. Or freeze on a tray in a single layer without touching, then transfer to a freezer-safe bag or container. To reheat, steam over boiling water for 5 to 8 minutes.

In China, dumplings filled with fish foretell a surplus of wealth for the eater.

Chinese siu mai (or Japanese shumai) are essentially open-face wontons, often served for dim sum. To form siu mai, roll out 3½-inch circles of Wonton Egg Wrapper Dough (page 26). Cup a wrapper in the palm of your hand. Place 1 teaspoon of filling in the center of the wrapper and lift the sides up around the filling, leaving the top exposed. Steam over boiling water until the dumplings are slightly translucent and the filling is entirely cooked.

JAPANESE PORK, CABBAGE & CHIVE GYOZA

MAKES ABOUT 24

Gyoza are traditional Japanese dumplings that are typically pan-fried. Their origin is rooted in China. This version of jiaozi was introduced to Japan by the Japanese occupiers of northeast China. Japanese touches may include utilizing garlic, sake, or sugar and using sesame oil for frying.

FILLING

1 pound ground pork

1½ cups shredded napa cabbage

½ cup finely chopped garlic chives or scallions

3 garlic cloves, grated

1 tablespoon soy sauce

1 tablespoon sake

2 teaspoons peeled, finely grated fresh ginger

1 teaspoon toasted sesame oil

½ teaspoon kosher salt

CONTINUED

WRAPPERS

Basic Asian Dumpling Dough (page 21) or
24 (3½ to 4-inch) round prepared wrappers

EXTRAS

1 tablespoon vegetable or sesame oil, for pan-frying

Tamari Dipping Sauce (page 50) and
Japanese hot mustard, for serving

To make the filling, combine the ingredients in a bowl and mix well. Cover and refrigerate for at least 30 minutes to allow the flavors to develop.

Roll out the dough as thin as possible, about ⅛ inch thick. Use a cookie cutter to cut into 3½ to 4-inch circles. Gather the dough scraps into a ball and roll again until all the dough is used.

Place about 1 tablespoon of the filling in the center of a wrapper and fold into a half-moon. Pinch or pleat the edges to seal. Line a tray with parchment paper or dust with flour. Set the dumpling on the tray and cover with plastic wrap or a damp towel to prevent it drying out. Repeat with the remaining filling and wrappers.

Heat the oil in a large skillet over medium-high heat. Arrange the gyoza in the pan, without overcrowding, sealed edges up. Pan-fry until golden brown on the bottom, 2 to 3 minutes. Carefully add ⅓ cup water to the pan (it will sizzle). Cover the skillet and decrease the heat to medium. Let the dumplings steam for 8 to 10 minutes. Remove the lid and continue to cook for 1 to 2 minutes more to evaporate any remaining moisture from the pan and until the gyoza are crisp.

Serve with Tamari Dipping Sauce and Japanese hot mustard.

Cooked gyoza can be stored in the refrigerator for up to 2 days or frozen for up to 2 months. Cool completely, then place in an airtight container, separated by parchment paper to prevent sticking. Or freeze on a tray in a single layer without touching, then transfer to a freezer-safe bag or container. To reheat, steam over boiling water for 5 to 8 minutes or pan-fry over medium heat to re-crisp and heat through, 3 to 5 minutes.

TAMARI DIPPING SAUCE

MAKES ABOUT 1 CUP

⅔ cup tamari
⅓ tablespoon unseasoned rice vinegar
1 teaspoon chili oil

Whisk together all the ingredients in a small bowl. Use immediately or store in the refrigerator for up to 3 days.

The Japanese proverb *Hana yori dango* translates to "dumplings rather than flowers," which implies a preference for substance (dumplings) over form (decorative ephemeral items such as flowers).

KOREAN KIMCHI & TOFU MANDU

MAKES ABOUT 24

Mandu are hearty, versatile dumplings introduced by the Yuan Mongolians in the fourteenth century. They symbolize prosperity and well-being and reinforce the three principles of Korean food: connection, balance, and nature. Mandu can be filled with meat or vegetables. They are boiled in soup, steamed, or pan- or deep-fried.

FILLING

1 (14-ounce package) firm tofu, pressed and crumbled

1 cup drained kimchi, finely chopped

¼ cup chopped scallions

2 shallots, minced

2 garlic cloves, grated

CONTINUED

2 tablespoons soy sauce or tamari

1 tablespoon peeled, finely grated fresh ginger

1 teaspoon toasted sesame oil

½ teaspoon kosher salt

WRAPPERS

Basic Asian Dumpling Dough (page 21) or 24 (3½ to 4-inch) round prepared wrappers

EXTRAS

1 tablespoon vegetable oil, for pan-frying

Mandu Dipping Sauce (page 54), soy sauce, and gochujang, for serving

To make the filling, combine the ingredients in a bowl.

Roll out the dough as thin as possible, about ⅛ inch thick. Use a cookie cutter to cut into 3½ to 4-inch circles. Gather the dough scraps into a ball and roll again until all the dough is used.

Place about 1 tablespoon of the filling in the center of a wrapper and fold into a half-moon. Pinch or pleat the edges to seal. Line a tray with parchment paper or dust with flour. Set the dumpling on the tray and cover with plastic wrap or a damp towel to prevent it drying out. Repeat with the remaining filling and wrappers.

Heat the oil in a large skillet over medium-high heat. Arrange the mandu in the pan without overcrowding. Pan-fry until golden on the bottom, 2 to 3 minutes. Carefully add 1/4 cup water to the pan (it will spatter). Cover the skillet and decrease the heat to medium. Steam for 2 to 3 minutes, then remove the lid and continue to cook until the water has evaporated.

Serve with Mandu Dipping Sauce or with soy sauce and gochujang.

Cooked mandu can be stored in the refrigerator for up to 2 days or frozen for up to 2 months. Cool completely, then refrigerate in an airtight container, separated by parchment paper to prevent sticking. Or freeze on a tray in a single layer without touching, then transfer to a freezer-safe bag or container. To reheat, use the original cooking method to pan-fry and steam over medium heat.

MANDU DIPPING SAUCE

MAKES ABOUT ¾ CUP

¼ cup soy sauce
¼ cup unseasoned rice vinegar
3 tablespoons water
1 garlic clove, grated
2 teaspoons packed light brown sugar
½ teaspoon toasted sesame oil
1 scallion, minced

Whisk together the ingredients in a small bowl. Use immediately or refrigerate for up to 1 day.

To press tofu, remove from the package and drain. Wrap with a kitchen towel or several layers of paper towels and place on a flat surface, such as a cutting board. Place a heavy object, such as a skillet, on top and press for at least 20 minutes.

Eating mandu during the Lunar New Year symbolizes wealth and fortune because their shape resembles old Korean coins and money pouches.

TIBETAN & NEPALESE BUFFALO MOMO

MAKES ABOUT 24

Momo originated in the Himalayan area of the Tibet region of China, where they were called "mog mog." They were introduced to Nepal by Tibetan migrants and traders. Momo are a staple in both Nepalese and Tibetan cuisine, where they are considered a cultural icon that represents a diverse community and rich culinary heritage. Momo are often filled with meat such as yak, pork, or chicken and vegetables and then steamed or fried and served with a spicy tomato chutney.

FILLING

1 pound ground buffalo (bison) or ground lean beef

½ small yellow onion, finely chopped

4 garlic cloves, minced

3 scallions, chopped

CONTINUED

¼ cup chopped fresh cilantro leaves

1 tablespoon peeled, finely grated fresh ginger

1 teaspoon kosher salt

1 teaspoon ground cumin

½ teaspoon ground coriander

¼ teaspoon turmeric

⅛ teaspoon cayenne

WRAPPERS

Basic Asian Dumpling Dough (page 21) or 24 (3½ to 4-inch) round prepared wrappers

EXTRAS

Tomato Pickle (page 58), for serving

To make the filling, combine the ingredients in a bowl.

Roll out the dough as thin as possible, about ⅛ inch thick. Use a cookie cutter to cut into 3½ to 4-inch circles. Gather the dough scraps into a ball and roll again until all the dough is used.

Place 1 tablespoon of the filling in the center of a wrapper and fold into a half-moon. Pinch and pleat the edges to seal. Line a tray with parchment paper or dust with flour. Set the dumpling on the tray and cover with plastic wrap or a damp towel to prevent it drying out. Repeat with the remaining filling and wrappers.

Fill a steamer with water. Grease the steamer basket with oil or line with parchment paper, lettuce leaves, or cabbage leaves to prevent sticking. Steam until fully cooked, 10 to 12 minutes. Serve with Tomato Pickle.

Cooked momo can be stored in the refrigerator for up to 2 days or frozen for up to 2 months. Cool completely, then refrigerate in an airtight container, separated by parchment paper to prevent sticking. Or freeze on a tray in a single layer without touching, then transfer to a freezer-safe bag or container. To reheat, steam over boiling water for 5 to 10 minutes.

TOMATO PICKLE

MAKES ABOUT 1½ CUPS

1 tablespoon vegetable oil
2 garlic cloves, chopped
1 to 2 dried red chiles
1 teaspoon peeled, finely grated fresh ginger
3 to 4 vine-ripened tomatoes, chopped
1 Sichuan pepper (optional)
Kosher salt and sugar

Heat the oil in a small saucepan over medium heat. Add the garlic, chiles, and ginger and sauté until fragrant, about 30 seconds. Add the tomatoes and the pepper, if using. Cook until the tomatoes break down, 5 to 7 minutes, stirring frequently. Transfer to a blender or food processor and process to blend. Season with the salt and sugar to taste.

INDIAN POTATO & PEAS SAMOSAS

MAKES 10 TO 12

Samosas are triangular pastries found throughout South Asia. It is believed that they originated in the Middle East in the ninth century. In India, samosas are a popular street food and are often served at festivals such as Diwali and Eid. They have a flaky dough wrapper that encases a meat or vegetarian filling and are often fried until golden brown. Samosas can also be baked. They are best served warm with a chutney, such as mint or tamarind, for dipping.

DOUGH

2 cups all-purpose flour

¾ teaspoon kosher salt

½ teaspoon ajwain seeds (optional)

3 tablespoons oil or melted butter or ghee

½ cup water

CONTINUED

FILLING

1 pound Yukon Gold potatoes, peeled and cut into 1-inch chunks

1 tablespoon vegetable oil, plus more for deep-frying

1 teaspoon cumin seeds

2 garlic cloves, minced

2 teaspoons peeled, finely grated fresh ginger

1 cup defrosted frozen peas

1 teaspoon garam masala

1 teaspoon ground coriander

½ teaspoon ground cumin

½ teaspoon turmeric

1 small green chile (such as jalapeño), seeded and finely chopped

1 teaspoon kosher salt

¼ cup finely chopped fresh cilantro leaves

To make the dough, combine the flour, salt, and ajwain seeds, if using, in a bowl. Add the oil. Using your fingers, rub the flour to incorporate the oil and to achieve a crumb consistency. Add the water a splash at a time until the dough comes together. Knead until slightly stiff but smooth and pliable. Cover with plastic wrap and let rest for 30 minutes.

Alternatively, use prepared samosa dough sheets, packaged phyllo dough, or packaged large spring roll wrappers for the samosa dough.

To make the filling, place the potatoes in a pot and cover with cold water. Bring to a boil and cook until very tender. Drain and mash.

Heat the 1 tablespoon vegetable oil in a skillet over medium heat. Stir in the cumin, garlic, and ginger and sauté until fragrant, about 30 seconds. Add the peas, garam masala, coriander, cumin, and turmeric and stir until fragrant, about 15 seconds. Add the potatoes, chile, and salt and and stir to thoroughly combine. Remove from the heat and stir in the cilantro.

Divide the dough into 10 to 12 equal portions. Lightly flour a work surface, then roll each portion into a thin strip, about 10 inches in length and 2½ to 3 inches in width.

Working with one strip at a time, fold up the narrow end on the diagonal, to form a triangle, and then fold again on the diagonal to form a pocket. Spoon the filling into the pocket without overstuffing. Continue to fold up on the diagonal to seal and form an enclosed triangle shape.

CONTINUED

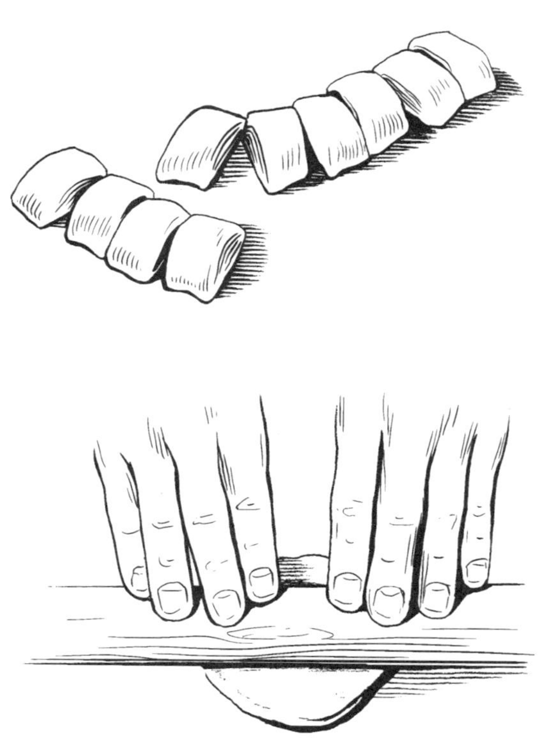

Line a tray with parchment paper or dust with flour. Set the samosa on the tray and cover with plastic wrap or a damp towel to prevent it drying out. Repeat with the remaining filling and dough.

Deep-fry or bake the samosas. To deep-fry, fill a pot, about one-third full, with vegetable oil. Heat to 350°F. Fry the samosas in batches until crisp and golden brown, 8 to 10 minutes; drain on paper towels. To bake, preheat the oven to 400°F. Lightly brush the samosas with oil and arrange on a baking sheet. Bake until golden brown and crispy, 12 to 15 minutes, turning once.

Cooked samosas can be stored in the refrigerator for up to 2 days or frozen for up to 1 month. Cool completely, then place in an airtight container, separated by paper towels to prevent sticking. Or freeze on a tray in a single layer without touching, then transfer to a freezer-safe bag or container. To reheat, place on a tray lined with parchment paper. Bake in a preheated 350°F oven for 10 to 15 minutes, flipping halfway through.

EURASIA & EUROPE

Food, in the end, in our own tradition, is something holy. It's not about nutrients and calories. It's about sharing. It's about honesty. It's about identity.

—LOUISE FRESCO

GEORGIAN KHINKALI

MAKES ABOUT 18

Khinkali are thick and meaty soup dumplings that are considered a national dish of Georgia. They were likely influenced by the momo dumpling of conquering Mongolians in the thirteenth century and the Asian culinary traditions shared along the Silk Road. Khinkali symbolize an offering to the sun. Their round shape resembles the sun, and the folds in the dough are considered a symbol of the sun's journey, with each fold representing a ray of the sun. Twenty folds are considered the minimum, and twenty-eight folds are ideal, representing the years of the solar cycle.

FILLING

12 ounces ground beef or ground lamb

1 small yellow onion, grated

¼ cup chopped cilantro leaves

2 garlic cloves, grated

CONTINUED

1 teaspoon kosher salt

1 teaspoon ground cumin

¼ teaspoon crushed red chile flakes, plus more for serving

½ cup water

WRAPPERS

Basic European Dumpling Dough (page 29)

EXTRAS

Freshly ground black pepper, for serving

2 bay leaves

To make the filling, combine all the ingredients except the water in a bowl. Add the water a little at a time until fully absorbed.

Roll the dough out to about ¼ inch thick. Use a cookie cutter to cut into 6-inch circles. Place about 1½ tablespoons of the filling in the center of the wrapper. Fold up the dough, pleating and folding the edges to enclose the filling. Twist and pinch the dough together at the top to seal and create a little handle or stem.

Line a tray with parchment paper or dust with flour. Set the dumpling on the tray and cover with plastic wrap or a damp towel to prevent it drying out. Repeat with the remaining filling and wrappers.

Fill a pot with water, add salt and the bay leaves, and bring to a boil over high heat. Add the dumplings in batches, without crowding the pot, stirring gently to prevent sticking. Gently boil until they float to the surface, about 8 minutes. Use a spider strainer to transfer to a plate.

Serve with freshly ground black pepper or crushed red chile flakes.

Cooked khinkali can be stored in the refrigerator for up to 2 days or frozen for up to 2 months. Cool completely, then refrigerate in an airtight container, separated by parchment paper to prevent sticking. Or freeze on a tray in a single layer without touching, then transfer to a freezer-safe bag or container. To reheat, steam over boiling water for 5 to 8 minutes.

SIBERIAN PELMENI

MAKES ABOUT 24

Pelmeni are a traditional Russian dumpling that originated in Siberia. It's believed that their origin traces back to the fifteenth century, when they were influenced by Chinese jiaozi, which were brought to Siberia by Mongolian settlers. Pelmeni *is derived from the Finno-Ugric word* pelm, *meaning "ear-shaped bread." These dumplings are filled with raw meat such as pork, beef, or lamb and then boiled or fried in butter. They are usually garnished with fresh dill and served with butter or sour cream.*

FILLING

8 ounces ground pork

8 ounces ground beef

1 small yellow onion, finely chopped

1 clove garlic, grated

1 teaspoon kosher salt

½ teaspoon black pepper

WRAPPERS

Basic European Dumpling Dough (page 29)

EXTRAS

Fresh dill, for garnish

Butter or sour cream, for serving

To make the filling, combine the ingredients in a bowl and mix without overworking.

Roll out the dough as thin as possible, about 1/8 inch thick. Use a cookier cutter to cut into 3½ to 4-inch circles. Gather the dough scraps into a ball and roll again until all the dough is used.

Place about 1 teaspoon of the filling in the center of a wrapper and fold into a half-moon. Pinch the edges tight to seal. Connect the two corners to form the classic pelmeni (or tortellini) shape. Line a tray with parchment paper or dust with flour. Set the dumpling on the tray and cover with plastic wrap or a damp towel to prevent it drying out. Repeat with the remaining filling and wrappers.

CONTINUED

Steam or boil the pelmeni. To steam, arrange in batches in a steamer basket over gently simmering water. Steam until tender, 8 to 10 minutes. To boil, fill a pot with water, add salt, and bring to a boil over high heat. Add the dumplings in batches, without crowding the pot, stirring gently to prevent sticking. Gently boil until they float to the surface, about 5 minutes. Use a spider strainer to transfer to a plate.

Garnish with fresh dill and serve with butter or sour cream.

Cooked pelmeni can be stored in the refrigerator for up to 2 days or frozen for up to 2 months. Cool completely, then refrigerate in an airtight container, separated by parchment paper to prevent sticking. Or freeze on a tray in a single layer without touching, then transfer to a freezer-safe bag or container. To reheat, steam over boiling water for 5 to 8 minutes.

POLISH MUSHROOM & SAUERKRAUT PIEROGI

MAKES ABOUT 24

Pierogi are a treasured national dish of Poland. They originated as an affordable means to feed a family during times of scarcity and remain a symbolic reminder of Polish resilience. With the passage of time, pierogi have evolved to be a beloved comfort food eaten at family gatherings and on holidays. Pierogi can be boiled, baked, or pan- or deep-fried. A flour dough encases a filling that can be savory with foraged wild mushrooms, sauerkraut, or potato or sweet with local berries.

FILLING

½ ounce dried porcini mushrooms

1 medium yellow onion, finely chopped

1 tablespoon unsalted butter

CONTINUED

8 ounces fresh mushrooms (such as portobello or cremini), washed, stemmed, and finely chopped

2 cups drained sauerkraut, chopped

2 to 3 tablespoons finely chopped fresh Italian parsley leaves

¾ teaspoon kosher salt

¼ teaspoon black pepper

WRAPPERS

Basic European Dumpling Dough (page 29) or Sour Cream Dumpling Dough (page 31)

EXTRAS

Melted butter and sour cream, for serving

To make the filling, soak the porcini mushrooms in hot water until soft, about 20 minutes. Drain and reserve the water. Squeeze the mushrooms dry and then finely chop.

Melt the butter in a skillet over medium heat. Add the onion and sauté until soft, about 3 minutes. Add the porcini and fresh mushrooms and sauté until any juices are released and the mushrooms take on color, about 5 minutes. Add the sauerkraut and cook until any moisture evaporates, stirring frequently.

Stir in the parsley, salt, and pepper and remove from the heat. Let cool.

Roll out the dough as thin as possible, about 1/8 inch thick. Use a cookie cutter to cut into 3½ to 4-inch circles. Gather the dough scraps into a ball and roll again until all the dough is used.

Place about 1 teaspoon of the filling in the center of a wrapper and fold into a half-moon. Pinch the edges tight to seal. Line a tray with parchment paper or dust with flour. Set the dumpling on the tray and cover with plastic wrap or a damp towel to prevent it drying out. Repeat with the remaining filling and wrappers.

Fill a large pot with water, add salt, and bring to a boil over high heat. Add the dumplings in batches, without crowding the pot, stirring gently to prevent sticking. Gently boil until they float to the surface, 3 to 4 minutes, then let them float for 1 to 2 minutes more. Use a spider strainer to transfer them to a plate. Toss with melted butter or quickly pan-fry in a skillet lightly coated with melted butter until golden and crisp, 3 to 4 minutes. Serve with sour cream.

CONTINUED

Cooked pierogi can be stored in the refrigerator for up to 2 days or frozen for up to 2 months. Cool completely, then refrigerate in an airtight container, separated by parchment paper to prevent sticking. Or freeze on a tray in a single layer without touching, then transfer to a freezer-safe bag or container. To reheat, use the original cooking method to boil, then pan-fry and steam over medium heat.

Ukrainian varenyky (vareniki) are very similar to Polish pierogi. They are also half-moon in shape and are usually boiled and filled with cheese curd, potato, or cabbage and served with sour cream.

ASHKENAZI BEEF KREPLACH

MAKES ABOUT 24

Kreplach are sometimes called Jewish wontons or ravioli. These dumplings have rich cultural and religious significance and are traditionally eaten during High Holidays and other holidays, such as Purim and Sukkot. Kreplach are believed to have originated in the fourteenth century, influenced by Italy's pasta-making tradition, which migrated from Venice to Germany, where it was adapted by Ashkenazi Jews. The term kreplach *is derived from Yiddish and means "meat dumpling." Kreplach can be made with leftover brisket, chicken, or chicken liver, vegetables, and onion.*

FILLING

1 tablespoon olive oil or schmaltz (rendered chicken fat)

1 small yellow onion, finely chopped

CONTINUED

2 garlic cloves, minced

12 ounces ground beef or ground chicken

1 teaspoon sweet paprika

½ teaspoon dried thyme

1 teaspoon kosher salt

½ teaspoon black pepper

WRAPPERS

Wonton Egg Wrapper Dough (page 26) or 24 (3 ½ to 4-inch) square prepared wrappers

EXTRAS

Fresh dill, for garnish

To make the filling, heat the oil in a large skillet over medium heat. Add the onion and sauté until soft and beginning to color, about 5 minutes. Add the garlic and stir until fragrant, about 15 seconds. Add the beef and cook, stirring to break up the pieces until the meat releases its juices. Continue to cook until the juices evaporate and the meat begins to brown. Stir in the paprika, thyme, salt, and pepper.

To make the wrappers, roll out the dough as thin as possible, about ⅛ inch thick. Cut into 2-inch squares. Gather the dough scraps into a ball and roll again until all the dough is used.

Place a spoonful of the filling in the center of a wrapper. Fold into a triangle and press the edges to seal. Line a tray with parchment paper or dust with flour. Set the dumpling on the tray and cover with plastic wrap or a damp towel to prevent it drying out. Repeat with the remaining filling and wrappers.

Fill a large pot with water, add salt, and bring to a boil over high heat. Add the dumplings in batches, without crowding the pot, stirring gently to prevent sticking. Gently boil until they float and begin to shrink around the filling, about 5 minutes. Remove with a spider strainer and drain. Then, if desired, pan-fry in a lightly oiled skillet until golden and crisp, 3 to 4 minutes. Alternatively, add the dumplings to a prepared chicken broth for a soup. Serve garnished with fresh dill.

Cooked kreplach can be stored in the refrigerator for up to 2 days or frozen for up to 2 months. Cool completely, then refrigerate in an airtight container, separated by parchment paper to prevent sticking. Or freeze on a tray in a single layer without touching, then transfer to a freezer-safe bag or container. To reheat, steam over boiling water for 5 to 8 minutes.

GERMAN & AUSTRIAN BLUEBERRY KNÖDEL

MAKES 8

Sweet and savory dumplings, or knödel, are a staple in German, Austrian, and Czech cuisine. Knödel are steamed yeast dumplings. These blueberry knödel are particularly common in regions such as the Black Forest and Bavaria, where wild blueberries are abundant and foraging for them is a popular pastime. Serve them with melted butter, cinnamon sugar, whipped cream, or vanilla sauce.

½ cup milk, lukewarm (100°F)

½ packet (4 grams) dry yeast, or 10 grams fresh yeast

3 tablespoons sugar, divided

2 cups all-purpose flour

¼ teaspoon kosher salt

1 large egg

2 tablespoons unsalted butter, melted

½ teaspoon vanilla extract

8 ounces fresh blueberries

Granulated sugar and finely grated lemon zest, for sprinkling

Melted butter, cinnamon sugar, whipped cream, or vanilla sauce, for serving

Combine the milk, yeast, and 1 tablespoon of the sugar in a bowl. Let stand at room temperature until bubbles form on the surface, about 5 minutes. Combine the flour, the remaining 2 tablespoons sugar, and the salt in a mixing bowl. Add the yeast mixture, egg, butter, and vanilla. Knead by hand or in a mixer fitted with a dough hook until smooth and elastic, about 8 to 12 minutes. Cover with a towel and let rest until doubled in size, about 1 hour.

Punch the dough down and divide into 8 equal portions. Slightly flatten each portion and place a spoonful of the blueberries in the center. Sprinkle with a scant teaspoon of sugar and a pinch of lemon zest.

CONTINUED

Wrap the dough around the berries and roll to make a smooth ball. Repeat with the remaining dough and berries. Cover with a towel and let rise for 15 to 20 minutes.

Fill a pot with water and bring to a boil over high heat. Place the dumplings in a steamer, decrease the heat, and steam over a gentle simmer until fluffy and cooked through, about 15 minutes. Serve warm with melted butter, cinnamon sugar, whipped cream, or vanilla sauce.

Cooked knödel can be stored in the refrigerator for up to 2 days or frozen for up to 1 month. Cool completely, then place in an airtight container, separated by paper towels to prevent sticking. Or freeze on a tray in a single layer without touching, then transfer to a freezer-safe bag or container. To reheat, steam in a steamer basket over boiling water for 10 to 15 minutes.

ITALIAN SPINACH & RICOTTA GNUDI

MAKES ABOUT 16

Italian cuisine includes a variety of popular stuffed dumplings such as ravioli and tortellini. Unstuffed dumplings are another style that includes gnocchi and gnudi. Gnudi are humble dumplings from the Tuscan countryside, where they are made with flour and ricotta from local sheep. Gnudi means "naked," which refers to their appearance without a pasta wrapper. Gnudi are often served with a tomato or brown butter sauce and are best served immediately once cooked.

12 ounces fresh baby spinach

12 ounces fresh ricotta, drained

1 large egg

¾ cup finely grated Parmigiano-Reggiano cheese, plus more for serving

⅓ cup all-purpose flour or Italian 00 flour

CONTINUED

½ teaspoon kosher salt

¼ teaspoon black pepper

½ teaspoon finely grated lemon zest

Pinch of nutmeg

EXTRAS

Butter Sauce (page 86), for serving

Steam the spinach until wilted, 3 to 4 minutes. Transfer to a colander and drain thoroughly, pressing out any excess liquid. Transfer to a cutting board and finely chop, continuing to squeeze out any liquid. Place the spinach in a bowl. Add the remaining ingredients and mix to combine.

Dust a baking tray with flour. Scoop 1 heaping tablespoon of the spinach mixture and shape into a 1½-inch ball. Place the gnudi on the tray, repeat with the remaining dough, and refrigerate for 30 minutes.

Fill a large pot with water and bring to a boil. Line a plate with paper towels. Add the dumplings in batches, without crowding the pot, stirring gently to prevent sticking. Gently boil until they float to the surface, 3 to 4 minutes, depending on their size. Remove with a spider strainer and place on the plate to drain. Transfer to a warm bowl and cover with a plate or lid to keep warm while you make the sauce.

Serve with Butter Sauce.

BUTTER SAUCE

MAKES ½ CUP

½ cup (1 stick) unsalted butter
4 to 6 sage sprigs
Pinch of kosher salt

Melt the butter in a small saucepan over medium heat. Add the sage and continue to cook until the butter turns golden brown in color. (Keep an eye on it, as it will brown quickly.) Season with the salt.

SWEDISH POTATO BACON KROPPKAKOR

MAKES 10 TO 12

Kroppkakor are mashed potato dumplings traditionally stuffed with pork, onions, and spices. Their rustic heartiness reflects Sweden's agricultural roots and resourcefulness, relying on simple, locally available ingredients. A common dish among farmers and rural communities, kroppkakor provided a nutritious and filling meal during long, dark winters. Today they play a role in Sweden's culinary heritage and are enjoyed throughout the country. They are often served with lingonberry preserves and sour cream.

2 pounds starchy potatoes, such as russet, peeled and cut into 1-inch chunks

1 cup all-purpose flour or potato flour

1 large egg plus 1 egg yolk

1 teaspoon kosher salt

CONTINUED

8 ounces bacon, coarsely chopped

1 small yellow onion, finely chopped

1 teaspoon ground allspice

¼ teaspoon white pepper

Lingonberry preserves and sour cream, for serving

Fill a pot with water, add salt, and bring to a boil over high heat. Add the potatoes and boil until tender. Drain and cool, then transfer to a bowl. Mash until smooth or push through a ricer. Add the flour, egg and egg yolk, and salt and stir to combine without overmixing. The dough should be soft but firm. Cover with plastic wrap and chill for 30 minutes.

Fry the bacon in a skillet over medium heat until the fat renders, 5 to 7 minutes. Add the onion and sauté until soft and golden in spots. Pour off any excess fat from the pan and discard. Return the pan to the heat and stir in the allspice and pepper. Remove from the heat and let cool.

Lightly flour a work surface. Divide the dough into 10 to 12 balls. Working with one dough ball at a time, press a finger into the center of the ball to create a pocket. Place about 1 tablespoon of the bacon mixture in the pocket. Pinch the edges of the dough to seal and gently roll into a smooth ball. Line a tray with parchment paper. Set the kroppkakor on the tray and cover with plastic wrap or a damp towel to prevent it drying out. Repeat with the remaining bacon mixture and dough.

Fill a large saucepan with water, lightly add salt, and bring to a boil over high heat. Add the dumplings in batches, without crowding the pot, stirring gently to prevent sticking. Gently boil until they float, 8 to 10 minutes. Then simmer for an additional 2 to 3 minutes. Remove with a spider strainer and transfer to a plate. Serve with lingonberry preserves and sour cream.

Cooked kroppkakor can be stored in the refrigerator for up to 2 days or frozen for up to 1 month. Cool completely, then place in an airtight container, separated by paper towels to prevent sticking. Or freeze on a tray in a single layer without touching, then transfer to a freezer-safe bag or container. To reheat cooked kroppkakor, gently boil, steam, or pan-fry in a skillet lightly coated with vegetable oil. Frozen uncooked kroppkakor should be boiled. (Note the cooking time will be slightly longer when frozen.)

Food for us comes from our relatives, whether they have wings or fins or roots. That is how we consider food. Food has a culture. It has a history. It has a story. It has relationships.

—WINONA LADUKE

MIDDLE EAST & AFRICA

The heritage of
the past is the
seed that brings
forth the harvest
of the future.

—WENDELL PHILLIPS

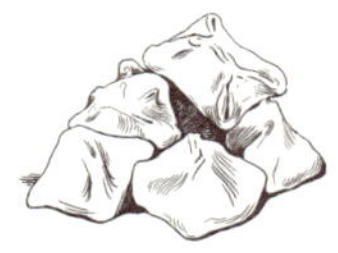

TURKISH MANTI WITH YOGURT SAUCE & TOMATO OIL

MAKES ABOUT 36

Manti are small, delicate dumplings stuffed with spiced ground meat such as lamb and served with a yogurt sauce. They are a staple of Turkish cuisine often prepared for special occasions and family gatherings and are a traditional feature in pre-wedding ceremonies. Manti are notably small and labor intensive, which often makes them a communal activity. It's considered that the smaller the dumpling, the more skilled the cook. Manti dough is firmer than other basic European dumpling doughs and usually does not include fat.

FILLING

12 ounces ground lamb or ground beef

1 small red onion, finely chopped or grated

CONTINUED

¼ cup chopped fresh mint leaves

2 tablespoons finely chopped Italian parsley leaves

¾ teaspoon kosher salt

½ teaspoon black pepper

¼ teaspoon sumac

WRAPPERS

Wonton Egg Wrapper Dough (page 26) or 36 (1-inch) square prepared wrappers

EXTRAS

Yogurt Sauce and Tomato Oil (pages 96 and 97), for serving

Fresh mint or sumac, for garnish

To make the filling, combine the ingredients in a bowl and gently mix to blend.

To make the wrappers, roll out the dough as thin as possible, ⅛ inch. Cut into 1-inch squares. Gather the dough scraps into a ball and roll again until all the dough is used.

Place a pea-sized amount of filling in the center of a wrapper. Pinch the opposite corners together to seal.

Line a tray with parchment paper or dust with flour. Set the dumpling on the tray and cover with plastic wrap or a damp towel to prevent it drying out. Repeat with the remaining filling and dough.

Fill a pot with water, add salt, and bring to a boil. Add the manti and simmer until they float, 8 to 10 minutes. Remove with a spider strainer to a plate and drain. Arrange on a serving plate. Spoon Yogurt Sauce over and around the manti and drizzle with Tomato Oil. Garnish with mint or sumac.

Cooked manti can be stored in the refrigerator for up to 2 days. Cool completely, then place in an airtight container, separated by parchment paper to prevent sticking. To reheat, steam over boiling water for 5 to 8 minutes.

YOGURT SAUCE

MAKES ABOUT 1 CUP

1 cup whole milk Greek yogurt
2 garlic cloves, grated
1 tablespoon olive oil
¼ teaspoon kosher salt

Combine the ingredients in a small bowl and mix to blend. Use immediately or store in the refrigerator for up to 1 day.

TOMATO OIL

MAKES ABOUT 5 TABLESPOONS

¼ cup olive oil
1 tablespoon tomato paste
1 teaspoon Aleppo pepper flakes or crushed red chile flakes
¼ teaspoon sumac
1 tablespoon finely chopped fresh mint leaves

Heat the oil in a small saucepan. Whisk in the tomato paste, Aleppo pepper flakes, and sumac. Simmer until fragrant, about 15 seconds. Remove from the heat and stir in the mint. Use immediately or store in the refrigerator for up to 1 day. Reheat in a saucepan over low heat before using.

SOUTH AFRICAN CINNAMON SOUSKLUITJIES

MAKES ABOUT 12

Souskluitjies are pillowy cinnamon-flavored dumplings introduced by the early Dutch settlers in the Cape of South Africa during the seventeenth century. Their name is derived from the Dutch words sous *(sauce) and* kluitjies *(dumplings). Over time they became a beloved Afrikaans dessert and a comforting and affordable staple of home-cooked meals. Souskluitjies are best served immediately once cooked.*

1 cup all-purpose flour

1 teaspoon baking powder

½ teaspoon kosher salt, divided

3 tablespoons plus 2 tablespoons unsalted butter, cold, cubed

2 large eggs, room temperature

¼ cup whole milk

½ teaspoon vanilla extract

¼ cup plus ½ cup sugar

2 teaspoons ground cinnamon, divided

Combine the flour, baking powder, and ¼ teaspoon of the salt in a bowl. Add the 3 tablespoons butter and rub the mixture with your fingertips to achieve a crumb consistency. Whisk together the eggs, milk, and vanilla in a separate bowl. Stir into the flour mixture to combine without overmixing.

Fill a large saucepan with 3 to 4 inches of water, add the remaining ¼ teaspoon salt, and bring to boil. Drop heaping tablespoons of the dough into the pot in batches without crowding the pot. Cover the pot and reduce the heat to a low boil. Simmer until the dumplings are cooked through, 8 to 10 minutes. (Do not remove the lid or the dumplings will flatten.)

While the dumplings are cooking, whisk the ¼ cup sugar and 1 teaspoon of the cinnamon in a small bowl and set aside for sprinkling.

CONTINUED

When the dumplings are ready, remove from the pot with a spider strainer and transfer to a plate. Lightly sprinkle with some of the cinnamon-sugar mixture. Repeat with the remaining dough. Reserve the cooking liquid for the sauce.

To make the sauce, combine 2 cups of the reserved cooking liquid with the remaining 2 tablespoons butter, ½ cup sugar, and 1 teaspoon cinnamon in a small saucepan. Bring to a boil, stirring to dissolve the sugar. Let boil until the liquid is slightly reduced, 3 to 4 minutes.

Spoon the dumplings into bowls. Serve with the sauce and the remaining cinnamon sugar for sprinkling.

I realized very early the power of food to evoke memory, to bring people together, to transport you to other places, and I wanted to be a part of that.

—JOSÉ ANDRÉS

AMERICAS

SWEET POTATO & POBLANO EMPANADAS

MAKES 10 TO 12

Empanadas are believed to have originated in the Galicia region of Spain, where the tradition of encasing a filling in pastry was likely influenced by Middle Eastern pastries (sambousek). The Spanish conquistadors brought empanadas to the Americas, where they became a staple in Argentinian and other Latin American cuisines as well as a feature during religious holidays, celebrations, and street festivals.

DOUGH

2¼ cups all-purpose flour

¼ cup masa harina (corn flour)

1 teaspoon kosher salt

½ cup (1 stick) unsalted butter, cold, diced

1 large egg

½ cup water, cold

CONTINUED

FILLING

1 tablespoon vegetable oil

½ small yellow onion, finely chopped (about ¼ cup)

1 medium poblano pepper, seeded and finely diced

3 garlic cloves, minced

2 teaspoons ground cumin

1 teaspoon sweet paprika

¼ teaspoon ground coriander

3 medium sweet potatoes, roasted whole, skins removed, and coarsely mashed (about 1½ cups)

½ cup canned black beans, drained

1 teaspoon kosher salt

¼ teaspoon black pepper

¼ cup chopped fresh cilantro leaves

1 egg whisked with 1 tablespoon water, for brushing

To make the dough, place the flour, masa harina, and salt in the bowl of a food processor. Pulse once or twice to blend. Add the butter and pulse until the mixture resembles peas. Add the egg and pulse until the mixture is crumbly. Drizzle in the water and pulse until the dough is shaggy and begins to come together.

Lightly flour a work surface. Transfer the dough to the work surface and knead for about 30 seconds. Shape the dough into a disk. Wrap in plastic wrap and refrigerate for at least 1 hour.

To make the filling, heat the oil in a large skillet over medium heat. Add the onion and sauté until soft, 3 to 4 minutes. Add the poblano and sauté until bright and crisp-tender, 1 to 2 minutes. Stir in the garlic, then stir in the cumin, paprika, and coriander. Stir in the sweet potatoes, beans, salt, and pepper and remove from the heat. Stir in the cilantro and let cool.

Divide the dough into 10 to 12 pieces. Lightly flour a work surface and roll each piece into a 5 to 6-inch circle, about ⅛ inch thick.

Place 2 tablespoons of the filling in the center of a dough circle. Brush the edges with the egg wash. Fold into a half-moon, seal the edges with your fingers, and crimp them with a fork. Line a tray with parchment paper or dust with flour. Set the empanada on the tray and cover with plastic wrap or a damp towel to prevent it drying out. Repeat with the remaining filling and dough.

CONTINUED

Preheat the oven to 400°F. Line a baking sheet with parchment paper.

Brush the empanadas with the egg wash and arrange on the baking sheet. Bake until golden brown, about 25 minutes, rotating the pan once.

Cooked empanadas can be stored in the refrigerator for up to 2 days or frozen for up to 2 months. Cool completely, then refrigerate in an airtight container, separated by parchment paper to prevent sticking. Or freeze on a tray in a single layer without touching, then transfer to a freezer-safe bag or container. To reheat unfrozen cooked empanadas, preheat your oven to 350°F and line a baking sheet with parchment paper. Arrange the empanadas on the sheet and bake for 10 to 15 minutes. To reheat frozen cooked empanadas, transfer directly from the freezer to a parchment-lined baking sheet and bake at 350°F for 20 to 25 minutes.

TAMALES

Tamales are wrapped bundles filled with corn dough (masa) and a savory or sweet filling. The dough is spread on corn husks or banana leaves, and the filling is spooned over it. The husks or leaves are wrapped up, tied, and then steamed until the masa is cooked.

Tamales are found throughout Latin America but are often associated with Mexican cuisine. Their history is traced to ancient Mesoamerican civilizations, including the Mayans, Aztecs, and Olmecs, as far back as 8000 BC. Tamales were considered sacred food of the gods and often used for ritual sacrifice. Today they are a central part of Latin American culture and history and a symbol of community, family, and celebration.

PARAGUAYAN VORI VORI

MAKES 16 TO 18 DUMPLINGS;
SERVES 4 TO 6 AS A SOUP

Vori vori is a comforting cornmeal dumpling soup that is a staple in everyday meals in Paraguay. Its origin can be traced to matzah ball soup, which originated in the Near East during the late antiquity period. The soup tradition was brought to the Americas by the conquistadors and was further reinforced by European Jews migrating to South America during the twentieth century.

DUMPLINGS

1¼ cups finely ground cornmeal or corn flour

½ cup whole milk ricotta, drained

¼ cup fresh mozzarella, shredded

1 large egg, lightly beaten

½ teaspoon kosher salt

EASY CHICKEN SOUP

1 small chicken or 2 bone-in split chicken breasts, rinsed

1 medium yellow onion, cut into 8 wedges

3 garlic cloves, chopped

2 carrots, peeled and sliced

2 celery stalks, sliced

Kosher salt and freshly ground black pepper

To make the dumplings, combine all the ingredients in a bowl, being careful not to overmix. Scoop 1 heaping tablespoon of the dough and roll it into a ball. Place on a plate and repeat with the remaining dough. Cover with plastic wrap and refrigerate until ready to use.

To make the soup, place the chicken, onion, and garlic in a large pot or Dutch oven. Add enough water to cover the chicken, 6 to 8 cups. Bring to a boil, then decrease the heat to low, cover the pot, and simmer for 1 hour. Remove the chicken from the pot and place on a cutting board to cool.

Add the carrots and celery to the pot, bring to a low boil, and simmer until the vegetables are bright and crisp-tender, 8 to 10 minutes.

CONTINUED

When the chicken is cool enough to handle, remove and discard the skin and bones. Shred the meat. Return the chicken meat to the pot and bring the soup back to a boil. Add the dumplings and simmer until they float to the top, 6 to 8 minutes. Season with the salt and pepper to taste before serving.

NATIVE AMERICAN GRAPE DUMPLINGS

Grape dumplings are a traditional food of Native American tribes, including Cherokee, Chickasaw, and Choctaw nations in the southeastern United States. The dumplings were originally made from cornmeal and cooked in a mash made from native purple muscadine grapes, known as possum grapes, or sour grapes that turn sweet only after a hard freeze. Today they are usually made with flour, sugar, and purple grape juice, and they remain a cherished dish that's often present at tribal events and festivals.

Food is our common ground, a universal experience.

—JAMES BEARD

METRIC CONVERSIONS & EQUIVALENTS

APPROXIMATE METRIC EQUIVALENTS

VOLUME

¼ teaspoon	1 milliliter
½ teaspoon	2.5 milliliters
¾ teaspoon	4 milliliters
1 teaspoon	5 milliliters
1¼ teaspoons	6 milliliters
1½ teaspoons	7.5 milliliters
1¾ teaspoons	8.5 milliliters
2 teaspoons	10 milliliters
1 tablespoon (½ fluid ounce)	15 milliliters
2 tablespoons (1 fluid ounce)	30 milliliters
¼ cup	60 milliliters
⅓ cup	80 milliliters
½ cup (4 fluid ounces)	120 milliliters
⅔ cup	160 milliliters
¾ cup	180 milliliters
1 cup (8 fluid ounces)	240 milliliters
1¼ cups	300 milliliters
1½ cups (12 fluid ounces)	360 milliliters
1⅔ cups	400 milliliters
2 cups (1 pint)	480 milliliters
3 cups	720 milliliters
4 cups (1 quart)	0.96 liter
1 quart plus ¼ cup	1 liter
4 quarts (1 gallon)	3.8 liters

MASS

1/4 ounce	7 grams
1/2 ounce	14 grams
3/4 ounce	21 grams
1 ounce	28 grams
1 1/4 ounces	35 grams
1 1/2 ounces	42.5 grams
1 2/3 ounces	47 grams
2 ounces	57 grams
3 ounces	85 grams
4 ounces (1/4 pound)	113 grams
5 ounces	142 grams
6 ounces	170 grams
7 ounces	198 grams
8 ounces (1/2 pound)	227 grams
16 ounces (1 pound)	454 grams
35.25 ounces (2.2 pounds)	1 kilogram

LENGTH

1/8 inch	3 millimeters
1/4 inch	6.25 millimeters
1/2 inch	1.25 centimeters
1 inch	2.5 centimeters
2 inches	5 centimeters
2 1/2 inches	6.25 centimeters
4 inches	10 centimeters
5 inches	12.75 centimeters
6 inches	15.25 centimeters
12 inches (1 foot)	30.5 centimeters

METRIC CONVERSION FORMULAS

TO CONVERT	MULTIPLY
Ounces to grams	Ounces by 28.35
Pounds to kilograms	Pounds by .454
Teaspoons to milliliters	Teaspoons by 4.93
Tablespoons to milliliters	Tablespoons by 14.79
Fluid ounces to milliliters	Fluid ounces by 29.57
Cups to milliliters	Cups by 240
Cups to liters	Cups by .236
Pints to liters	Pints by .473
Quarts to liters	Quarts by .946
Gallons to liters	Gallons by 3.785
Inches to centimeters	Inches by 2.54

OVEN TEMPERATURES

To convert Fahrenheit to Celsius, subtract 32 from Fahrenheit, multiply the result by 5, then divide by 9.

DESC.	FAHRENHEIT	CELSIUS	BRITISH GAS MARK
Very cool	200°	95°	0
Very cool	225°	110°	¼
Very cool	250°	120°	½
Cool	275°	135°	1
Cool	300°	150°	2
Warm	325°	165°	3
Moderate	350°	175°	4
Moderately hot	375°	190°	5
Fairly hot	400°	200°	6
Hot	425°	220°	7
Very hot	450°	230°	8
Very hot	475°	245°	9

COMMON INGREDIENTS & THEIR APPROXIMATE EQUIVALENTS

1 cup uncooked white rice = 185 grams
1 cup all-purpose flour = 120 grams
1 stick butter (4 ounces • ½ cup • 8 tablespoons) = 110 grams
1 cup butter (8 ounces • 2 sticks • 16 tablespoons) = 220 grams
1 cup brown sugar, firmly packed = 213 grams
1 cup granulated sugar = 200 grams

Information compiled from a variety of sources, including *Recipes Into Type* by Joan Whitman and Dolores Simon (Newton, MA: Biscuit Books, 1993); *The New Food Lover's Companion* by Sharon Tyler Herbst (Hauppauge, NY: Barron's, 2013); and *Rosemary Brown's Big Kitchen Instruction Book* (Kansas City, MO: Andrews McMeel, 1998).

ABOUT THE AUTHOR

Lynda Balslev is an award-winning cookbook author and food and drinks writer who is passionate about sharing her knowledge through the lens of travel and culture. Lynda is the author of six books, including *Almonds: Recipes, History, Culture* and *The Little Book of Fika*. She currently writes a nationally syndicated food column and blog: *TasteFood*. Her work has appeared in various print and digital media, including NPR, *Culture*, *EatingWell*, *Relish*, and *Parade Magazine*.

The authorised representative in the EEA is Simon and Schuster Netherlands BV, Herculesplein 96 3584 AA Utrecht, Netherlands. (info@simonandschuster.nl)

Andrews McMeel Publishing
a division of Andrews McMeel Universal
1130 Walnut Street, Kansas City, Missouri 64106

www.andrewsmcmeel.com

26 27 28 29 30 TEN 10 9 8 7 6 5 4 3 2 1

ISBN: 979-8-8816-0557-5

Library of Congress Control Number: 2025936819

Editor: Jean Z. Lucas
Designer: Brittany Lee
Production Editor: Kayla Overbey
Production Manager: Chadd Keim
Illustrations: Joe McKendry & Adobe Stock